Survival Chinese Lessons

生存汉语

Joann Pittman
English Language Institute/China
2010

Survival Chinese Lessons

生存汉语

Joann Pittman
English Language Institute/China

ISBN: 978-1-93565-112-3

Cover and Interior Design by Arnold Molina
Photos by Joann Pittman

Printed in the United States of America

2 3 4 5 6 7 8 / 14 13 12 11

Contents

Introduction

In 1582 an Italian Jesuit named Matteo Ricci arrived in Macau to begin learning the Chinese language. He would eventually master the language and come to be recognized as a true Chinese scholar by the intellectual elite of the day. He not only spoke the language fluently; he translated the Confucian classics into Latin, and even wrote books in Chinese himself.

After establishing communities in Macau, Guangzhou, Nanchang, and Nanjing, he was granted permission by the emperor to live in Beijing in 1601, becoming the first westerner to reside there. He died at his home in Beijing in 1610.

In march 2010, to mark the 400th anniversary of his death the municipal government of his hometown in Italy sponsored a special exhibition on his life and work at the Beijing Capital Museum, titled *"Matteo Ricci: An Encounter of Civilizations in Ming China."* The exhibit included many 16th century artifacts, including original Chinese language books written by Ricci.

One section of the exhibit focused on his years of language study in Macau, and was titled "In the Whirlpool of the Chinese Language." It's an apt description of what it's like for "foreigners" to learn Chinese.

Many people come to China with the hope and/or intention of learning the language, but soon give up. The tones, the unfamiliar sounds, the complexity of the characters quickly form themselves into a whirling mass that overwhelms the motivation and desire to learn. The task seems too big.

Learning Chinese is a big task, but learning how to use the language to accomplish simple, everyday tasks is not. You may never, like Matteo Ricci, translate Chinese classics or write books in Chinese yourself. But even Ricci had to start with the basics, learning the sounds, the tones, and the simple vocabulary to accomplish stuff of everyday life.

And there-in lies the purpose of the book—to help you learn the sounds of Chinese as well as some basic vocabulary, questions, statements, and conversations. It is by no means a comprehensive Chinese language textbook. You will NOT be fluent by the time you work through it. Rather it is something to help you get your feet – or should I say your big toe – wet. Actually, if you can use this material when you are done, you will have just enough Chinese to get you into trouble.

Whether you' re trying to learn some Chinese in preparation for visit to China, for a short-term work assignment, or as the first steps in a life-long language learning journey, it is my hope that these materials will be helpful to you.

Special thanks to Zhu Hui for assistance in the recording.

Joann Pittman
July, 2010
Beijing, China

Components

Pinyin and Sound Chart

This section contains a brief explanation of the Pinyin Romanization of Chinese, and a chart of all the syllables used in the language.

Lessons

There are 15 lessons. In each lesson you will find basic phrases and vocabulary, as well as notes, a practice conversation, and some tips for learning.

CD / Audio Files

The phrases, vocabulary lists, and practice conversations are on the Survival Chinese CD. Listening is the most important first step in learning a language (it' s how you learned your own), so it is important to listen a lot. So do some listening activity everyday. The CD also includes the audio files for the sound chart.

Learning the Material

The best way to learn this material is to work with a language partner at least twice per week, listening a lot and practicing a lot.

If you are using this material before you go to China, and do not have a language partner, plan to spend most of your time listening to the material, familiarizing yourself with the sounds of Chinese.

The Sounds of Chinese: Pinyin

Pinyin is a system of writing the sounds of Chinese using English letters. It is fairly straight-forward, with each letter or group of letters corresponding exactly to a sound represented. Unlike English, there are no exceptions. Once you get it, you will have all you need to write down any sound you hear. The good news is that there are only 413 (or so) syllable sounds (consonant-vowel combinations.) If that scares you, remember that in English there are thousands of different consonant-vowel combinations.

For those of us who use non-character-based languages, Pinyin is a valuable tool to teach us how to say the language correctly. Since the correspondences between sound and writing are exact and unchanging, there's never any confusion as to how to pronounce a word written in Pinyin. And again, there are only 413 syllables (or 404, depending on how you count), so when you've learned how to say those correctly, you've learned how to "say" Chinese.

And now for the bad news: Certain English letters are attached to sounds that they are not associated with in English, so it takes a bit of "re-education" to learn what sounds they represent. For example, q is used to represent a sound that would be written with "ch" in English, and x is used to represent a sound that would be written with "sh".

The Beginnings

A. The following initial sounds are the same in both English and Chinese: b, d, f, g, h, j, k, l, m, p, s, t, w, y

B. The following initial sounds are different: (English has some of the sounds, but not at the beginning of words, only at the end)

z = a dz sound, as in suds

c = ts sound, as in cats

zh = a heavy j sound, as in John, jug, jog

ch = a heavy ch sound, as in church

sh = a heavy sh sound, as in shop

r = a heavy r sound, strongly emphasizing the beginning of really

q = a light ch sound (cheek)

x = a light sh sound (she)

The Simple Endings

Following are the simple endings on Chinese words:

a = like the *ahh* you say when the doctor tells you to "open wide"

an = like the English word *on*

ang = like most people pronounce Hong Kong

e = like ugh, without the *gh*

en = like the *un* in *undo*

eng = like the *ung* in *hung*

i = like *ee*, as in *sheep*. When it follows *zh*, *ch*, *sh*, or *r* – it is pronounced somewhat like an *r*. When it follows *z*, *c*, and *s*, it is not pronounced at all.

in = like *keen*, not *kin*

ing = like the sound in *sing*

o = like *aw*, as in *law*

ong = like *wrong* or *song*, especially if you are from New Jersey!

u = there are two pronunciations: *u* and *ü*. Normally, it is pronounced like the English word, *you*. When it follows *y*, *j*, *q*, or *x*, it is pronounced like English *u*, but your lips are pursed like you are going to kiss someone, and it has a nasal sound.

un = like *w+hewn* (no equivalent in English)

ün = similar to the *une* in June, with very pursed lips

The Complex Endings

Following are the complex endings to Chinese words:

ao = like the *ow* in *cow*

ei = like the *ay* sound in *pay*

ia = like the cowboy saying "*yee-ahh*", real fast!

ian = like the Japanese money *yen*

iang = like saying a long *e*, + *ong* as in wrong

iao = like when you are excited and say *yowzer*!

ie = like a New Yorker would say "*yeh*"

iu = like the English *you*

ua = like the English *wah*

uai = like the English word *why*, without the *h* sound

uan = like saying the Spanish name *Juan*, without the guttural at the front

ui = like saying the English word *way* very fast

uo = like someone from New Jersey saying *water*

ue = a rounded u, quickly followed by an *e* sound,

9

as in the word *set* or *pet*

uan = a rounded *u*, quickly followed by a sound like you are pronouncing the letter "n"

Some Troublemakers

Following are some of the trickier endings to Chinese words:

i = when followed by *z*, *c*, *s*, *zh*, *ch*, *sh*, and *r*, this ending is not an ending at all. There is no real vowel sound that it is representing. It's like "grr" in English.

er = one strange sound that is unique to itself. In certain dialects (Beijing) it is often tagged on to the end of words.

u and ü = learning these is a matter of remembering which sound follows which beginnings. There are only 6 sounds that can be followed by *ü*: *n*, *l*, *j*, *q*, *x* and *y*. Every beginning can be followed by *u* except *j*, *q*, *x*, *y*. Therefore, *n* and *l* can be followed by either.

Some Suggestions for working on Pinyin Pronunciation

1. Make it a matter of priority. Do not adopt the attitude that clear pronunciation is unimportant so long as you get the

message across. **Your goal in language learning is to speak the language *correctly*, not simply to speak it.**

2. Listen a lot. Pronunciation and listening are two sides of the same coin. You must be able to hear a sound correctly in order to pronounce it correctly.

3. Dictation: have your language partner say a list of 15 or 20 words and you write them down.

4. Prepare a list of words. Have your language partner read them to you randomly and you point to them.

5. Mimic: Choose a text. Have your language partner read the text, phrase by phrase, while you repeat after him/her.

6. Record: Have your language record a list of words or a text. Later, transcribe the list.

Tones

Each of the syllables or sounds can be said using four different tones. The first tone is a high flat tone, designated by the marker ¯ . The second tone is a rising tone, designated by the marker ´ . The third tone is a dipping tone, designated by the marker ˇ . The fourth tone is a falling tone, designated by the marker ` . There is also a neutral tone, which means that the syllable is unstressed. Neutral tones are only found in the second or third syllables of two or three-syllable words. Unlike English, where tones convey emotion and nuanced meaning, in Chinese they are an integral part of the meaning of the word. If you change the tone on a sound, it changes the word (*mā* = mother; *mǎ* = horse). Contrary to what many English speakers think (and hope), tones are <u>not optional</u>!!!

Problem Areas:
- 2nd tone. Many English speakers have difficulty with the second tone. We do have an equivalent, though, such as when you hear something that befuddles you and you say "huh??"
- Tone combinations. Particularly troublesome are 1st to 4th, and 3rd to 2nd. It takes constant repetition and concentration to consistently say these tone combinations correctly.

Some Suggestions for Working on Tones
1. Word Dictation. Have your language partner read words, and you write them down, marking the tones.

2. Sentence and phrase dictation. Have your language partner read sentences to you, and you write down the words and tones.

3. Have your language partner record words and sentences. You listen and transcribe, marking the tones.

4. Make a tone chart. It should have 20 columns or sections (or 20 separate pages). Each column should be for words of a particular tone, or tone combination. For example, you would have a column of all the 1st tone words you have learned or are learning, one for the 2nd tone words, one for the 3rd tone words, and one for the and 4th tones. Also, make columns for two-character words that have tone combinations (1-1, 1-2, 2-3, 3-4, etc.) As you learn words, add them to the appropriate columns. Then when your language partner comes, you have ready made lists from which to construct drills.

The Sound Chart

This is the bottom line – where it all begins. On this chart you will find all the sounds (syllables) in Chinese. This is it. Every word in Chinese is made up of one, two, or three of these sounds in combination. It's not particularly interesting, but you need to spend time working on these in order to be on the road to speaking Chinese correctly. Once you learn these sounds, you will have everything you need to be able to say Chinese words correctly.

The chart is divided into 4 sections, grouped according to vowel sounds.

Group I

a	o	e	-i	er	ai	ei	ao	ou	an	en	ang	eng	ong
ba	bo				bai	bei	bao		ban	ben	bang	beng	
pa	po				pai	pei	pao	pou	pan	pen	pang	peng	
ma	mo	me			mai	mei	mao	mou	man	men	mang	meng	
fa	fo					fei		fou	fan	fen	fang	feng	
da		de			dai	dei	dao	dou	dan	den	dang	deng	dong
ta		te			tai		tao	tou	tan		tang	teng	tong
na		ne			nai	nei	nao	nou	nan	nen	nang	neng	nong
la		le			lai	lei	lao	lou	lan		lang	leng	long
za		ze	zi		zai	zei	zao	zou	zan	zen	zang	zeng	zong
ca		ce	ci		cai		cao	cou	can	cen	cang	ceng	cong

s	zh	ch	sh	r	g	k	h	
song	zhong	chong		rong	gong	kong	hong	
seng	zheng	cheng	sheng	reng	geng	keng	heng	**eng**
sang	zhang	chang	shang	rang	gang	kang	hang	**ang**
sen	zhen	chen	shen	ren	gen	ken	hen	**en**
san	zhan	chan	shan	ran	gan	kan	han	**an**
sou	zhou	chou	shou	rou	gou	kou	hou	**ou**
sao	zhao	chao	shao	rao	gao	kao	hao	**ao**
	zhei		shei		gei	kei	hei	**ei**
sai	zhai	chai	shai		gai	kai	hai	**ai**
								er
si	zhi	chi	shi	ri				
se	zhe	che	she	re	ge	ke	he	**e**
								o
sa	zha	cha	sha		ga	ka	ha	**a**

Group II

i	ia	iao	ie	iu	ian	in	iang	ing	iong
bi		biao	bie		bian	bin		bing	
pi		piao	pie		pian	pin		ping	
mi		miao	mie	miu	mian	min		ming	
di		diao	die	diu	dian				
ti		tiao	tie		tian			ting	
ni		niao	nie	niu	nian	nin	niang	ning	
li	lia	liao	lie	liu	lian	lin	liang	ling	
ji	jia	jiao	jie	jiu	jian	jin	jiang	jing	jiong
qi	qia	qiao	qie	qiu	qian	qin	qiang	qing	qiong
xi	xia	xiao	xie	xiu	xian	xin	xiang	xing	xiong
yi	ya	yao	ye	you	yan	yin	yang	ying	yong

Group III

u	ua	uo	uai	ui	uan	un	uang	eng
bu								
pu								
mu								
fu								
du		duo		dui	duan	dun		
tu		tuo		tui	tuan	tun		
nu		nuo			nuan			
lu		luo			luan	lun		
zu		zuo		zui	zuan	zun		
cu		cuo		cui	cuan	cun		

18

su		suo		sui	suan	sun		
zhu		zhuo		zhui	zhuan	zhun	zhuang	
chu		chuo		chui	chuan	chun	chuang	
shu		shuo		shui	shuan	shun	shuang	
ru		ruo		rui	ruan	run		
gu	gua	guo	guai	gui	guan	gun	guang	
ku	kua	kuo	kuai	kui	kuan	kun	kuang	
hu	hua	huo	huai	hui	huan	hun	huang	
wu	wa	wo	wai	wei	wan	wen	wang	weng

Group IV

ü	ue	uan	un
nü	nue		
lü	lue		
jü	jue	juan	jün
qü	que	quan	qün
xü	xue	xuan	xün
yü	yue	yuan	yün

Techniques and Strategies

It is best to work on the sound chart with your language partner, and since it's big and laborious, work on it daily, for short periods of time. Below are some techniques and strategies that will help you make use of the sound chart to improve your pronunciation.

1. Highlight particularly troublesome sounds and focus on those for a day or a week.

2. Mimic. Have your language partner read a column or row, and you repeat.

3. For each of the groups of sounds, have your language

partner randomly say a sound and you point to it.

4. Have your language partner randomly point to a sound and you say it. Focus on the ones that you are having trouble with.

5. Read a column or row, asking your language partner to correct your pronunciation.

6.Practice saying each of sounds with the 4 different tones.

Lesson 1

Hi and Bye

Objective: to learn the most common ways to greet and say good-bye

Greetings:

1. nǐ hǎo	你好	hello
2. nín hǎo	您好	hello (polite)

Good-byes:

1. zài jiàn	再见	good-bye
2. míng tiān jiàn	明天见	see you tomorrow
3. màn zǒu	慢走	take care（"go slow"）

Vocabulary:

1. nǐ	你	you (singular)
2. hǎo	好	good; well
3. nín	您	you (formal, polite)
4. zài jiàn	再见	good-bye (lit: see you again)
5. míng tiān	明天	tomorrow
6. jiàn	见	to see
7. màn zǒu	慢走	go slow (take care)

Notes:

1. *nǐ hǎo* is the best known greeting. It literally means "you good". Many people have learned *nǐ hǎo ma* as a greeting, but this is not commonly used since it is more of a direct question meaning "how are you?" or "are you good."

2. *nín* is the polite, or honorific form of the 2nd person pronoun. It should be used when talking with people who are clearly older, or are of a higher social status than you.

3. *màn zǒu* is said to someone who is leaving, not to a person who is staying. Don't use it when you are leaving a friend's home. Say it when a friend is leaving your home.

4. Traditionally, people greeted one another by saying *nǐ chī fàn le ma?* (Have you eaten yet?) While still commonly used in the countryside or among older people, it is not used as much in the cities today.

Practice:

Dialogue 1

    A. nǐ hǎo   A. 你好。

    B. nǐ hǎo   B. 你好。

    A. zài jiàn   A. 再见。

    B. zài jiàn   B. 再见。

Dialogue 2

    A. nǐ hǎo   A. 你好。

    B. nǐ hǎo   B. 你好。

    A. zài jiàn   A. 再见。

    B. zài jiàn   B. 再见。

    A. màn zǒu   A. 慢走。

Dialogue 3

    A. nǐ hǎo   A. 你好。

    B. nǐ hǎo   B. 你好。

    A. míng tiān jiàn   A. 明天见。

    B. míng tiān jiàn   B. 明天见。

    A. màn zǒu   A. 慢走。

Lesson 2

Many Thanks

Objective: to learn how to express and respond to thanks

Below are some common ways of expressing and responding to thanks:

Expressing Thanks:

1. xiè xiè	谢谢	Thanks. (most common)
2. xiè xiè nǐ	谢谢你	Thank you. (more polite)
3. duō xiè	多谢	Many thanks.

Responding to Thanks:

1. bú xiè	不谢	Don't thank me.
2. bú yòng xiè	不用谢	No need to thank me.
3. méi guānxī	没关系	It doesn't matter. It's nothing.
4. méi shì	没事	It doesn't matter.

Vocabulary:

1. xiè	谢	thanks
2. duō	多	many / much
3. bù	不	no, not

4. yòng	用	need
5. méi	没	no, not (have)
6. guānxī	关系	relationship
7. shì	事	matter

Notes:

Chinese does not have an equivalent of "You're welcome" to receive thanks. In order to demonstrate modesty and humility, expressions of thanks are deflected, not received. If someone thanks you in Chinese, be sure to use one of the above expressions in your response.

Practice:

Dialogue 1

    A. xiè xiè nǐ.   A. 谢谢你。

    B. bú yòng xiè.   B. 不用谢。

Dialogue 2

    A. xiè xiè.   A. 谢谢。

    B. bú yòng xiè.   B. 不用谢。

Dialogue 3

    A. xiè xiè nǐ.   A. 谢谢你。

    B. méi guānxī   B. 没关系。

Dialogue 4

    A. duō xiè   A. 多谢。

    B. méi shì   B. 没事。

Dialogue 5

    A. nǐ hǎo   A. 你好。

    B. nǐ hǎo   B. 你好。

    A. xiè xiè nǐ   A. 谢谢你。

    B. bú xiè   B. 不谢。

    A. zài jiàn   A. 再见。

    B. zài jiàn   B. 再见。

Expansion Activity:

1. Ask your language partner to teach you other ways of saying and responding to thanks.

2. Whenever you are shopping in a market or involved in interactions with Chinese people, be sure to say thanks, and then make note of the response.

Lesson 3

Talking About Your Language

Objective: to learn a few self-defense phrases

Some Survival Phrases:

1. wǒ tīng bù dǒng   我听不懂。   I don't understand.
2. wǒ bú huì shuō   我不会说汉语。   I am not able to speak
    hànyǔ   Chinese.

Vocabulary:

1. wǒ	我	I, me
2. tīng	听	hear
3. bù	不	no; not
4. dǒng	懂	understand
5. huì	会	able; can
6. shuō	说	speak; talk
7. hànyǔ	汉语	Chinese language

Notes:

According to the dictionary, *bù* is a fourth tone word; however, the tone changes depending upon the tone of the word that follows it. If it is followed by a fourth tone word, then the tone of *bù* changes to a second tone. So *bù huì* becomes *bú huì*.

Practice:
Dialogue 1

A. nǐ hǎo	A. 你好。
B. wǒ bú huì shuō hànyǔ	B. 我不会说汉语。
A. zài jiàn	A. 再见。
B. zài jiàn	B. 再见。
A. màn zǒu	A. 慢走。
B. xiè xiè	B. 谢谢。

Dialogue 2

A. nǐ hǎo	A. 你好。
B. wǒ tīng bù dǒng	B. 我听不懂。
A. zài jiàn	A. 再见。
B. zài jiàn	B. 再见。
A. màn zǒu	A. 慢走。
B. màn zǒu	B. 慢走。

Expansion:

1. With your language partner, learn how to say some of the
   following phrases:
   A. How do you say...in Chinese?
   B. Please say it again.
   C. Did I say it correctly?
   D. Do you speak English?

2. There are a variety of terms used in Chinese to refer to the
   Chinese language. *hàn yǔ* is only one of them. With your
   language partner, learn the following other terms that mean
   "Chinese language". Find out from him/her what the
   differences and distinctions are between the terms. Practice
   each of them using the *wǒ bú huì*...pattern:

   zhōng guó huà   中国话
   zhōng wén   中文
   guó yǔ   国语

Lesson 4

Pronouns

Objective: to learn the Chinese Pronouns

Pronouns are one of the major building blocks of any language.
Chinese pronouns are actually easier than their English
counterparts. Whereas English has 11, Chinese only has 6 (not
including the possessive form).

The Chinese Pronouns:

1. wǒ	我	I, me
2. wǒ mén	我们	we, us
3. nǐ	你	you
4. nǐ mén	你们	you (plural)
5. tā	他 / 她 / 它	he / she / it
6. tā mén	他们 / 她们 / 它们	they, them
7. wǒ de / wǒ mén de	我的 / 我们的	my, mine
8. nǐ de / nǐ mén de	你的 / 你们的	your, yours
9. tā de / tā mén de	他的 / 她的 / 它的	
	他们的 / 她们的 / 它们的	
		his, hers, its, theirs

Notes:

1. There is only one third person (spoken) pronoun covering he, she, it. In written Chinese, each has it's own character, but, each is pronounced "ta". This is one reason you will find many Chinese confusing he/she when speaking English. They'll tend to refer to their husband as "she" or their wife as 'he". They are not used to making that distinction when speaking.

2. To make the pronoun plural, add the suffix -*men*.

3. The possessive form is made by adding yet another suffix (-*de*) to either the singular or plural form.

4. There is no distinction made between the subject form of the pronoun and the object form. For example, *tā* is he and him, she and her.

Lesson 5

What's in a Name?

Objective: to learn how to speak about and give your name

Asking about a person's name:

1. nín guì xìng?　您贵姓？　What is your family name?
2. nǐ jiào shén me 你叫什么名字？ What is your name?
   míng zi?　　　　　What are you called?

Stating your name:

1. wǒ xìng…　　　我姓……　　My family name is...
2. wǒ jiào…　　　我叫……　　My name is.../ I am
   　　　　　　　　　　　called...
3. wǒ de míng zi 我的名字叫　My name is.../ I am
   jiào…　　　　　……　　　called...

Vocabulary:

1. guì　　　贵　　precious, honored
2. xìng　　　姓　　family name; surname
3. jiào　　　叫　　to be called
4. míng zi　　名字　　given name

34

Notes:

1. The question, *nǐ jiào shén me míng zi* is used to learn what the person is called or what he/she goes by. If you' re talking to an adult, use it after you have already established what their family name is and now you want to know what you should call them. It is also the question you should use when inquiring about the name of a child, or someone who is clearly younger than you are.

2. In Chinese, the family name comes before the given name, and is more important than the given name. When talking to or about a person, refer to them by their family name, with a title after it.

3. Putting the *guì* before *xìng* is a way of bestowing honor on the person you are asking.

Practice:

Dialogue 1

A. nǐ hǎo.

B. nǐ hǎo.

A. nǐ jiào shén me míng zi?

B. wǒ jiào zhōu níng. nǐ ne?

A. wǒ jiào hé lín. zài jiàn.

B. zài jiàn.

A. màn zǒu.

B. xiè xiè.

Dialogue 2

A. nǐ hǎo.

B. nǐ hǎo.

A. nín guì xìng?

B. wǒ xìng zhōu. nín ne?

A. wǒ xìng hé. zài jiàn.

B. zài jiàn.

A. màn zǒu.

B. xiè xiè nín.

A. 你好。

B. 你好。

A. 你叫什么名字？

B. 我叫周宁。你呢？

A. 我叫荷林。再见。

B. 再见。

A. 慢走。

B. 谢谢。

A. 你好。

B. 你好。

A. 您贵姓？

B. 我姓周。您呢？

A. 我姓荷。再见。

B. 再见。

A. 慢走。

B. 谢谢您。

Expansion Activity:

1. Ask your language partner to help you find a suitable
   Chinese name. Try to stay away from a name that is merely
   a translation of your English name. To a Chinese person,
   it will sound funny, and may not have any meaning. The
   meanings of names are significant, so try to choose one that
   describes something about your personality or your values.
   Ask your Chinese friends or students if it "sounds"
   Chinese!

2. Ask your language partner to teach you 5 of the most
   common titles that you are likely to use. (e.g. Mr., Mrs.,
   Miss., Teacher, etc...)

Lesson 6

Are You American?

Objective: to learn how to state your nationality

Questions:

1. nǐ shì nǎ guó 你是哪国人？ What nationality are you?
   rén?

2. nǐ cóng nǎr 你从哪儿来？ Where are you from?
   lái?

3. nǐ shì měi guó 你是美国人吗？ Are you American?
   rén ma?

Responses:

1. wǒ shì měi guó 我是美国人。 I am American.
   rén.

2. wǒ cóng měi guó 我从美国来。 I am from America.
   lái.

3. shì. wǒ shì měi 是。我是美国 Yes. I am American.
   guórén. 人。

4. bú shì. wǒ bú shì 不是。我不是美 No, I am not
   měi guó rén. wǒ 国人。我是加拿 American. I am
   shì jiā ná dà rén. 大人。 Canadian.

38

Vocabulary:

1. shì	是	is / are / to be
2. nǎ	哪	which
3. guó	国	country; nation
4. cóng	从	from
5. nǎr	哪儿	where
6. lái	来	come
7. ma	吗	question particle
8. jiā ná dà	加拿大	Canada
9. měi guó	美国	United States
10. zhōng guó	中国	China

Notes:

1. The Chinese verb *shì* more or less carries the meaning of the English "to be". However, it is far less common. *shì* can be considered an equal sign between two nouns. It demonstrates the relationship between two nouns. For example, in the sentence, *tā shì lǎo shī* (He is a teacher), the *shì* describes the first noun with the second noun. English also has this usage, as witnessed by the English for the example sentence, but English also uses "is" to link nouns or pronouns with adjectives (Susan is tall. They are smart.), something which Chinese does not do. Therefore, some sentences in English

that use "to be" cannot be translated using *shì*. Also notice that, where English has three forms of "to be" (is, am, are), depending on which noun is used, Chinese only has one, *shì*.

2. The way to state a nationality is to put the word for person (*rén*) on the end of the word that names the country. The word for "America" is *měi guó*. The word for "American" is *měi guó rén*.

Practice:

Dialogue 1

    A. nǐ shì nǎ guó rén?   A. 你是哪国人？

    B. wó shì měi guó rén.   B. 我是美国人。

Dialogue 2

    A. nǐ cóng nǎr lái?   A. 你从哪儿来？

    B. wǒ cóng měi guó lái.   B. 我从美国来。

Dialogue 3

    A. nǐ shì měi guó rén ma?   A. 你是美国人吗？

    B. Shì. wǒ shì měi guó   B. 是。我是美国人。
       rén.

Dialogue 4

A. nǐ shì měi guó rén ma?

B. Bú shì. wǒ bú shì měi guó rén. wǒ shì jiā ná dà rén.

A. 你是美国人吗？

B. 不是。我不是美国人。我是加拿大人。

Dialogue 5

A. nǐ hǎo.

B. nǐ hǎo.

A. nǐ jiào shénme míng zi?

B. Wǒ jiào zhōu níng. nín ne?

A. wǒ jiào hé lín. nǐ shì nǎ guó rén?

B. wǒ shì měi guó rén. nǐ ne?

A. wǒ shì zhōng guó rén. zài jiàn.

B. zài jiàn. màn zǒu.

A. xiè xiè.

A. 你好。

B. 你好。

A. 你叫什么名字？

B. 我叫周宁。您呢？

A. 我叫荷林。你是哪国人？

B. 我是美国人。你呢？

A. 我是中国人。再见。

B. 再见。慢走。

A. 谢谢。

41

Lesson 7

This and That

Objective: to learn how to ask about and identify objects

Learning how to use two small words (this and that) can help immensely in your language learning. Among other things, it can help push you towards that "critical point" of using the language to learn the language. If you can say "What is this?" or "What is that?", you can turn every market excursion into a vocabulary building session.

Some Questions:

1. zhè shì shén me?	这是什么？	What is this?
2. nà shì shén me?	那是什么？	What is that?
3. zhè shì bǐ ma?	这是笔吗？	Is this a pen?
4. nà shì shū ma?	那是书吗？	Is that a book?
5. zhè shì bú shì bǐ?	这是不是笔？	Is this a pen?
6. nà shì bú shì shū?	那是不是书？	Is that a book?

Some Responses:

1. zhè shì bǐ.	这是笔。	This is a pen.
2. nà shì shū.	那是书。	That is a book.

3. shì. zhè shì bǐ.	是。这是笔。	Yes. This is a pen.
4. bú shì. nà bú shì shū.	不是。那不是书。	No. That is not a book.

Vocabulary:

1. zhè	这	this
2. nà	那	that
3. shū	书	book
4. bǐ	笔	pen
5. zhè ge / nà ge	这个 / 那个	this / that

Notes:

1. The placement of the question word "what" is different from English. Whereas in English, the question word is almost always at the front of the sentence, in Chinese it is usually at the end of the sentence. The actual rule is quite simple: the question word goes in the same position as the answer. So, if you are trying to identify an object (this is a book), the question would be phrased as "this is what?"

2. *ma* is a question particle that is placed at the end of a sentence to turn it into a yes/no question. Unlike English, there is no change in the word order of the sentence when it

43

becomes a question.

| This is a book. | *zhè shì shū.* |
| Is this a book? | *zhè shì shū ma?* |

3. A second way of forming a yes/no question is to add *bú shì* after the verb *shì*, so that it literally reads "is no is".

| This is a book. | *zhè shì shū.* |
| Is this a book? | *zhè shì bú shì shū?* |

4. The response to a yes/no question is either *shì* (is) or *bú shì* (not is). In general, the response is a re-statement of the verb (whether it is "is" or some other verb), in either the positive or negative form.

Techniques and Strategies

Use this pattern to learn some of the items in your house. Before your language partner comes, pull out 10 household items you want to learn. Use the following procedure:

· Listen as your language partner identifies all the objects, using the pattern, *zhè shì…*

- Ask identification questions for all the objects, using the pattern, *zhè shì shén me*? After your language partner gives the answer, repeat it.

- Have your language partner point to objects and ask you questions using the pattern, *zhè shì shén* me? or *zhè shì* (name) *ma*? You answer.

- Vocabulary is best learned in sets or categories. This pattern is helpful in using Chinese to learn vocabulary sets, such as vegetables, fruits, clothing items, etc.

Expansion Activity:
Go with your language partner to the market or department store and use this pattern to learn vocabulary sets.

Lesson 8

Count On It

Objective: to learn how to count in Chinese

Chinese numbers are not very difficult. Once you know the numbers 1-10, you have all you need to know to go to one hundred. There's no funny stuff like our English "-teen" or "-ty" to tack on the end of a number. Every number above ten is a combination of ten and another number.

1 to 10:   **The teens:**

yī	一	1		shí yī	十一	11
èr	二	2		shí èr	十二	12
sān	三	3		shí sān	十三	13
sì	四	4		shí sì	十四	14
wǔ	五	5		shí wǔ	十五	15
liù	六	6		shí liù	十六	16
qī	七	7		shí qī	十七	17
bā	八	8		shí bā	十八	18
jiǔ	九	9		shí jiǔ	十九	19
shí	十	10				

46

The Tens: **Higher Numbers:**

èr shí	二十	20		bǎi	百	100
sān shí	三十	30		qiān	千	1000
sì shí	四十	40		wàn	万	10,000
wǔ shí	五十	50				
liù shí	六十	60				
qī shí	七十	70				
bā shí	八十	80				
jiǔ shí	九十	90				

Techniques and Strategies:

1. Make a chart with the numbers 1-100 on it. With your language partner, you can do the following activities:
   · Your language partner says a number and you point to it.
   · You point to a number and your language partner says it. You repeat.
   · You say a number and your language partner points to it.

2. Have your language partner say random numbers, and you write them down. Try to increase the speed at which you can do this.

3. Identify important phone numbers and learn how to say them

Expansion Activities:

1. Asking about and giving phone numbers. Use the following Q/A patterns to learn how to ask about and give a phone number:

Q: *nǐ de diàn huà hào mǎ shì duō shǎo?* (Your telephone number is what?)

A: *wǒ de diàn huà hào mǎ shì 366-3542.* (My telephone number is 366-3542)

2. Before your language partner arrives, write out a list of phone numbers. Have your language partner ask you the above question, and you respond, using the list of phone numbers.

Lesson 9

How Old Are You?

Objective: to learn to ask for and give information about ages

People in China often find it difficult to judge the age of foreigners, so are quite eager to ask about your age. There are several different ways of asking a person's age, depending on the relative age (to you) of the person you are asking.

For children under the age of 10:

nǐ jǐ suì le?	你几岁了？	How old are you?
nǐ duō dà le?	你多大了？	How old are you?

For youngsters over 10 and adults:

nǐ duō dà le?	你多大了？	How old are you?
nín duō dà le?	您多大了？	How old are you?

For elderly people:

Nín duō dà nián jì le?	您多大年纪了？	How old are you?

The response to the question looks like this:

wǒ + number + *suì*

Wǒ sān shí sān suì.　我三十三岁。　　I am 33 years old.

Vocabulary:

1. jǐ	几	how many / how much?
2. suì	岁	age
3. le	了	sentence particle
4. duō dà	多大	how old?
5. nián jì	年级	age (years)

Notes:

1. Questions and statements about age do not include the verb "to be" (*shì*). The sentence is simply *the pronoun + age*.

2. Even though *jǐ* and *duō dà* have the same meaning, they are not necessarily interchangeable. *duō dà* cannot precede the word *suì*. *jǐ* cannot precede the word *nián jì*.

3. Don't use *nín* if you are talking to someone significantly younger than you, unless their status or position is clearly higher than yours (school president, government official).

Practice:

Dialogue 1

   A. nǐ jǐ suì le?   A. 你几岁了？

   B. Wǒ bā suì le.   B. 我八岁了。

Dialogue 2

   A. nǐ duō dà le?   A. 你多大了？

   B. Wǒ èr shí suì le.   B. 我二十岁了。

Dialogue 3

   A. nín duō dà nián jì le?   A. 您多大年纪了？

   B. Wǒ qī shí liù suì.   B. 我七十六岁。

Dialogue 4

   A. nǐ hǎo.   A. 你好。

   B. nǐ hǎo.   B. 你好。

   A. nín guì xìng?   A. 您贵姓？

   B. wǒ xìng zhōu.   B. 我姓周。

   A. nǐ shì nǎ guó rén?   A. 你是哪国人？

   B. wǒ shì měi guó rén.   B. 我是美国人。

   A. nǐ duō dà le?   A. 你多大了？

   B. sì shí qī suì. zài jiàn.   B. 四十七岁。再见。

   A. zài jiān.   A. 再见。

Expansion Activity:

When your language partner arrives, get out a picture of your family. Have your language partner ask the ages of your family members, and you respond.

Lesson 10

Dollars and Sense

Objective: to learn some vocabulary and patterns related to money

Figuring out what to call Chinese money can be very confusing because there are numerous words used to refer to money. The official name of the Chinese money is *rén mín bì*, which literally means "The People's Money." It is most commonly used in formal and/or written settings, but rarely used in spoken settings.

The basic unit of measure for Chinese money is *yuán*. If it helps, you can think of it as a Chinese dollar. This is the character you will on item price tags. Sometimes when a price is spoken, the word *yuán* will be used, but most often in spoken Chinese the word *kuài* is used. This literally means "lump" and can best be thought of as being a translation of "buck." *Kuài* is simply an informal way of saying *yuán*.

A Chinese *yuán* is divided into 100 *fēn*, like a cent. A *jiǎo* is 10 *fēn*, so it is similar to a US dime. Like the word *yuán*, however, *jiǎo* is mostly used in written Chinese. *Máo* is the spoken form of *jiǎo*.

The biggest difference from English is that when stating a price, Chinese counts the units of *jiǎo* (*máo*) as opposed to *fēn*. So, 1.50 is said as *yí kuài wǔ máo* (1 *kuài*, 5 *máo*, not 1 *kuài* 50 *fēn*).

Basic Vocabulary:

1. yuán	元	Chinese dollar
2. kuài	块	Chinese dollar (spoken)
3. jiǎo	角	10 Chinese cents
4. máo	毛	10 Chinese cents (spoken)
5. fēn	分	1 Chinese cent
6. qián	钱	money
7. rén mín bì	人民币	"The People's Money"
8. liǎng	两	2 of something (couple)
9. zhè ge	这个	this
10. nà ge	那个	that

When putting the vocabulary together to say a price, the pattern goes like this:

number + *kuài* + number + (*máo*) + (number) + (*fēn*) + (*qián*)

Some Examples:

1. yī kuài bā (máo qián)	一块八毛钱	1.80
2. liǎng kuài yī (máo qián)	两块一毛钱	2.10
3. sì kuài wǔ máo sān	四块五毛三	4.53
4. jiǔ shí jiǔ kuài jiǔ máo jiǔ	九十九块九毛九	99.99
5. wǔ kuài èr	五块二	5.20

Asking the price is done like this:

Duō shǎo qián?　　多少钱？　　How much does it cost?

Notes:

1. There are 2 words for dollar (*yuán and kuài*) and 2 words for ten cents, or a dime (*jiǎo* and *máo*). The second in each pair listed above is used much more in spoken Chinese. The first in each pair is used on price tags and in other written forms.

2. *liǎng* is another word for "2", and should be used whenever talking about two of something (2 dollars, 2 oranges, 2 books, etc.). It is not used in counting. You can think of it as meaning "a couple" (of something).

3. Saying *qián* is optional, as is the final *máo* and *fēn*. A basic

rule is that if another number comes after *máo* (4.53), then *máo* must be said.

Practice:

Dialogue

A. nǐ hǎo.

B. nǐ hǎo.

A. zhège duō shǎo qián?

B. sān kuài wǔ.

A. nà ge duō shǎo qián?

B. liù kuài.

A. xiè xiè. zài jiàn.

B. bú xiè. zài jiàn.

A. 你好。

B. 你好。

A. 这个多少钱？

B. 三块五。

A. 那个多少钱？

B. 六块。

A. 谢谢。再见。

B. 不谢。再见。

Techniques and Strategies:

1. Make a chart with a list of prices on it. With your language partner, you can do the following activities:

   · Your language partner says a price and you point to it.

   · You point to a price and your language partner says it. You repeat.

   · You say a price and your language partner points to it.

2. Have your language partner say random prices, and you

write them down. Try to increase the speed at which you can do this.

Expansion Activity:

1. Spend some time in a store or market, just asking prices. It gives you real-live practice, as well as a chance to strengthen your listening comprehension.

2. Ask your language partner to teach you some basic bargaining phrases.

Lesson 11

What Time Is It?

Objective: asking about and giving information regarding time

The Chinese way of asking the time and the English way are quite different. Chinese uses neither the question word "what," nor the word "time".

Asking the time:

The way to ask about the time is this:

Xiàn zài jǐ diǎn　　　现在几点　　　What time is it?

For your purposes here, it doesn't really matter what the individual words in this question mean, only that the question as a whole means "What time is it?"

The response looks like this:

xiàn zài + number + *diǎn* + (*fēn*) + (*zhōng*)

Here are some examples:

1. yī diǎn zhōng　　　　　一点钟　　　1:00
2. liǎng diǎn zhōng　　　　两点钟　　　2:00

3. sān diǎn zhōng	三点钟	3:00
4. sì diǎn zhōng	四点钟	4:00
5. wǔ diǎn zhōng	五点钟	5:00
6. liù diǎn zhōng	六点钟	6:00
7. qī diǎn zhōng	七点钟	7:00
8. bā diǎn zhōng	八点钟	8:00
9. jiǔ diǎn zhōng	九点钟	9:00
10. shí diǎn zhōng	十点钟	10:00
11. shí yī diǎn zhōng	十一点钟	11:00
12. shí èr diǎn zhōng	十二点钟	12:00

The half hours are said like this:

1. yī diǎn bàn	一点半	1:30
2. liǎng diǎn bàn	两点半	2:30
3. sān diǎn bàn	三点半	3:30
4. sì diǎn bàn	四点半	4:30
5. wǔ diǎn bàn	五点半	5:30
6. liù diǎn bàn	六点半	6:30
7. qī diǎn bàn	七点半	7:30
8. bā diǎn bàn	八点半	8:30
9. jiǔ diǎn bàn	九点半	9:30
10. shí diǎn bàn	十点半	10:30
11. shí yī diǎn bàn	十一点半	11:30
12. shí èr diǎn bàn	十二点半	12:30

Vocabulary:

1. xiàn zài	现在	now; at present
2. diǎn	点	point; "o'clock"
3. zhōng	钟	clock
4. bàn	半	half
5. fēn	分	minute
6. shàng wǔ	上午	morning (AM)
8. xià wǔ	下午	afternoon (PM)

Other times are said like this:

1. yī diǎn shí fēn	一点十分	1:10
2. liǎng diǎn shí wǔ fēn	两点十五分	2:15
3. sān diǎn èr shí fēn	三点二十分	3:20
4. sì diǎn èr shí wǔ fēn	四点二十五分	4:25
5. wǔ diǎn sān shí wǔ fēn	五点三十五分	5:35

Practice:
Dialogue

A. nǐ hǎo.	A. 你好。
B. nǐ hǎo.	B. 你好。
A. xiàn zài jǐ diǎn?	A. 现在几点？
B. sān diǎn bàn.	B. 三点半。
A. xiè xiè. zài jiàn.	A. 谢谢。再见。
B. bú xiè. zài jiàn.	B. 不谢。再见。

Notes:

1. To identify AM or PM, put the word *shàng wǔ* (morning) or *xià wǔ* (afternoon) <u>before</u> the time phrase. 8:00 AM would be *shàng wǔ bā diǎn*. 8:00 PM would be *xià wǔ bā diǎn*.

2. The time phrase is <u>always</u> placed at the beginning of the sentence, immediately before or after the subject. This is because Chinese has no verb tense markers, so it is important to establish up front when the action is taking place.

Techniques and Strategies:

1. Make a chart with the times on it. With your language partner, you can do the following activities:
   - Your language partner says a time and you point to it.
   - You point to a time and your language partner says it. You repeat.
   - You say a time and your language partner points to it.

2. Have your language partner say random times, and you write them down. Try to increase the speed at which you can do this.

3. Repeat the practice conversation above, substituting different times.

Expansion Activities:

1. Before your language partner arrives, make a list of 10 of your daily activities.

2. With your language partner, learn how to say the various activities.

3. Then, make statements about what time you do each activity during the day.

4. For example, the way to say "get up" is *qǐ chúang*. A statement about the time you get up would look like this: *wǒ liù diǎn qǐ chúang* (I get up at 6:00, or literally I at 6:00 get up.)

Lesson 12

Day to Day

Objective: to learn how to identify the days of the week

Unlike English, which has a different name for each day of the
week, Chinese simply assigns numbers to the days of the week.
Take the word for week (*xīngqī*) and add the number 1 to it,
and you have "Monday."

Days of the week:

1. xīng qī yī   星期一   Monday
2. xīng qī èr   星期二   Tuesday
3. xīng qī sān   星期三   Wednesday
4. xīng qī sì   星期四   Thursday
5. xīng qī wǔ   星期五   Friday
6. xīng qī liù   星期六   Saturday
7. xīng qī tiān   星期天   Sunday

Identifying Relative Days:

1. dà qián tiān   大前天   two days ago
2. qián tiān   前天   the day before yesterday
3. zuó tiān   昨天   yesterday

4. jīn tiān	今天	today
5. míng tiān	明天	tomorrow
6. hòu tiān	后天	the day after tomorrow
7. dà hòu tiān	大后天	two days from now

Asking Answering Questions:

Q. jīn tiān xīng qī jǐ?	今天星期几?	What day is it today?
A. jīn tiān xīng qī wǔ.	今天星期五。	Today is Friday.
Q. míng tiān xīng qī jǐ?	明天星期几?	What day is it tomorrow?
A. míng tiān xīng qī tiān.	明天星期天。	Tomorrow is Sunday.

Notes:

1. When making statements about days, there is no need to include the verb "to be". It is implied.

Techniques and Strategies:

1. Have your language partner say the names of the days, as you write them down.

2. Get out a calendar. With your language partner, do the

64

following activities:
- You point to a day and your language partner says it.
- Your language partner says a day and you point to it.
- You say a day and your language partner points to it.

Expansion Activity:

Before your language partner arrives, make a list of 10 (weekly) activities (going to the market, going to the bank, cooking supper, watching TV, etc.). With your language partner, learn how to say those 10 activities. Then make statements about what day you do each activity:

wǒ xīng qī sān kàn diànshì.   On Wednesdays I watch TV.
(I Wednesday watch TV.)

Remember that the time phrase <u>always</u> precedes the verb phrase because there are no tense markers.

Lesson 13

Month By Month

Objective: to learn the months of the year

Identifying months in Chinese is actually quite simple since months don't have special names as they do in English. The word for "month" is *yuè*. The name of the month is formed by saying a number + the word *yuè*.

The Months:

1. yī yuè (fēn)   一月   January
2. èr yuè   二月   February
3. sān yuè   三月   March
4. sì yuè   四月   April
5. wǔ yuè   五月   May
6. liù yuè   六月   June
7. qī yuè   七月   July
8. bā yuè   八月   August
9. jiǔ yuè   九月   September
10. shí yuè   十月   October
11. shí yī yuè   十一月   November
12. shí èr yuè   十二月   December

Relative Months:

1. shàng shàng ge yuè   上上个月   the month before last
2. shàng ge yuè   上个月   last month
3. zhè ge yuè   这个月   this month
4. xià ge yuè   下个月   next month
5. xià xià ge yuè   下下个月   the month after next

Identifying Dates:

wǔ yuè sì hào   五月四号   May 4

shí yuè yī hào   十月一号   October 1

shí èr yuè èr shí wǔ hào   十二月二十五号   December 25

Notes:

1. *shàng* means "up" and *xià* means "down", so "last month" is the month above this month and "next month" is the month below this month. This is a reflection of traditional Chinese calendars, which were usually arranged in a vertical format, reading from the top down.

2. *gè* is a measure word. Measure words precede nouns and are generally used in identification or counting phrases. Each noun has a particular measure word assigned to it, but *gè* is sort of a generic one that can be attached to most

nouns as a default if you don' t know the real one. There are dozens of different measure words, so it' s good to learn the accompanying measure word when you learn a noun.

3. *hào* is a word for number.

Techniques and Strategies:

1. Have a calendar ready for when your language partner arrives.
   - Your language partner says a time and you point to it.
   - You point to a time and your language partner says it. You repeat.
   - You say a time and your language partner points to it.

2. Have your language partner say random dates, and you write them down. Try to increase the speed at which you can do this.

Expansion Activities:

1. Work with your language partner to learn how to ask and answer the following questions:
   - In what month were your born? What date?
   - In what month did you come to China? What date?
   - In what month will you go to Thailand? What date?

2. Ask your language partner to teach you how to say the years.

Lesson 14

Taxi! Taxi!

Objective: to learn the basics of giving directions to taxi drivers

Basic Instructions:

1. wǒ yào qù…	我要去······	I want to go to...
2. wǎng yòu guǎi	往右拐	Turn right.
3. wǎng zuǒ guǎi	往左拐	Turn left.
4. yī zhí zǒu	一直走	Go straight.
5. zài zhèr tíng chē	在这儿停车	Stop the car here.
6. qǐng kāi fā piào	请开发票	Please give a receipt.
7. nǐ qù nǎr?	你去哪儿?	Where are you going?
		Where do you want to go?

Vocabulary:

1. wǎng	往	towards; in the direction of
2. yòu	右	right
3. zuǒ	左	left
4. guǎi	拐	turn
5. yī zhí	一直	straight ahead
6. zǒu	走	to go
7. zài	在	at

8. zhèr / nàr	这儿 / 那儿	here / there
9. tíng	停	stop
10. chē	车	car; vehicle
11. qǐng	请	please
12. kāi	开	prepare; write
13. fā piào	发票	receipt
14. qù	去	to go in the direction of
15. nǎr	哪儿	where
16. bīn guǎn	宾馆	hotel

Notes:

1. Notice that in statements #2, 3, 4 above, the directional phrase (*wǎng yòu*) comes before the verb.

2. Notice that in statement #5, the phrase describing the location (*zài zhèr*) comes before the verb.

Practice:

Dialogue

A. nǐ háo.　　　　　　　A. 你好。

B. nǐ hǎo.　　　　　　　B. 你好。

A. nǐ qù nǎr?　　　　　　A. 你去哪儿？

B. wǒ qù bīn guǎn…yī zhí　　B. 我去宾馆……一直
　　zǒu…wǎng yòu guǎi…　　　走……往右拐……

71

wǎng zuǒ guǎi…zài zhèr   往左拐……在这儿停

tíng chē. qǐng kāi fāpiào.   车。请开发票。

xiè xiè.   谢谢。

A. bú xiè. màn zǒu.   A. 不谢。慢走。

B. zài jiàn.   B. 再见。

Techniques and Strategies:

1. Go for a walk with your language partner. Have her/him give you simple directions in Chinese (turn right, turn left) and you follow them.

2. Reverse roles. You give instructions to your language partner and have him/her follow them.

Expansion Activities:

1. Ask your language partner to teach you how to say some of the following locational phrases:
   - at the intersection
   - at the traffic light
   - at the corner
   - at the gate

2. Work with your language partner to learn the names of 5 key locations in the city where you live.

Lesson 15

I Want Food!

Objective: to learn the names of basic market foods

Some Common Food Items:

1. xī guā   西瓜   watermelon
2. píng guǒ   苹果   apple
3. xiāng jiāo   香蕉   banana
4. miàn bāo   面包   bread
5. mǐ fàn   米饭   rice
6. huā shēng   花生   peanuts
7. tǔ dòu   土豆   potato
8. jī dàn   鸡蛋   egg
9. chá   茶   tea
10. yǐn liào   饮料   soft drink / soda pop
11. niú nǎi   牛奶   milk
12. niú ròu   牛肉   beef
13. jī ròu   鸡肉   chicken
14. zhū ròu   猪肉   pork
15. jīn   斤   Chinese pound (1.1 lbs)

The basic patterns to use when you want to buy something are the following:

| 1. *wǒ yào …* | 我要…… | I want... |
| 2. *wǒ bú yào…* | 我不要…… | I don't want... |

The basic question patterns asking if you want something are the following:

| 1. *nǐ yào shén me?* | 你要什么？ | What do you want? |
| 2. *nǐ yào bú yào…* | 你要不要……？ | Do you want..." |

Practice:

Dialogue

A. nǐ háo	A. 你好。
B. nǐ hǎo	B. 你好。
A. nǐ yào shénme?	A. 你要什么？
B. wǒ yào píng guǒ. Píng guǒ duō shǎo qián?	B. 我要苹果。苹果多少钱？
A. sān máo qián yī jīn.	A. 三毛钱一斤。
B. wǒ yào yī jīn. xiè xiè. zài jiàn.	B. 我要一斤。谢谢。再见。
A. bú xiè. zài jiàn.	A. 不谢。 再见。

Expansion Activity:

With your language partner, learn the names of 10 other common foods.

Lesson 16

"What'll You Have?"

Objective: to learn some basic phrases and vocabulary for eating in a restaurant

Whether a gymnasisum-sized hall where waiters are dashing about on roller skates or the neighborhood 'hole-in-the-wall" Chinese restaurants serve some of the best food on the planet. Since eating in a restaurant can be quite cheap, many foreign visitors and residents of China find themselves eating out a lot.

Vocabulary:

diǎn	点	to order
jǐ	几	how many?
wèi	位	formal measure word for people
xiǎng	想	want to / desire to
chī	吃	eat
hē	喝	drink
wǎn	碗	bowl
bēi	杯	cup / glass
dǎ bāo	打包	pack up (a 'doggy bag')

mǎi dān	买单	the bill / the check
jiē zhàng	结账	calculate the bill /check
chá	茶	tea
gōng bào jī dīng	宫爆鸡丁	"kung pao chicken" (spicy chicken with peanuts)

Some basic patterns you will use in a restaurant:

| *jǐ wèi?* | 几位？ | How many people? |

(You respond with the number + weì.)

The waiter or waitress will use the following patterns to ask what you want to order:

Nǐ diǎn shénme?	你点什么？	What do you want to order?
Nǐ xiǎng chī shénme?	你想吃什么？	What do you want to eat?
Nǐ xiǎng hē shénme?	你想喝什么？	What do you want to drink?

You respond with the following

wǒ diǎn + the name of the dish you want to order.

我点……

wǒ xiǎng chī + the name of the dish you want to order.
我想吃……

wǒ xiǎng hē + the name of the drink you want to order.
我想喝……

Practice:

Dialogue:

A. jǐ wèi?	A. 几位？
B. sān wèi.	B. 三位。
A. nǐmen diǎn shénme?	A. 你们点什么？
B. wǒmen diǎn gōng bào jī dīng.	B. 我们点宫爆鸡丁。
A. nǐmen xiǎng hē shénme?	A. 你们想喝什么？
B. wǒmen xiǎng hē chá.	B. 我们想喝茶。
……	……
B. qǐng mǎi dān.	B. 请买单。
A. hǎo. dǎ bāo ma?	A. 好。打包吗？
B. dǎ bāo.	B. 打包。

Notes:

· In a situation like this, *xiǎng* and *yào* are interchangeable. They both convey the meaning of 'want to.'

78

- Menus at big restaurants usually have photographs; but be aware that beef and beef stomach look very similar in a picture.
- Water is not served unless it is ordered. If you want 'cold' water, it will be bottled, and it will not be free. 'Free' water will be simply a cup of hot boiled water.

APPENDIX A: Some Menu Items

These tend to be favorites of foreigners.

糖醋里脊	Táng cù lǐ jǐ	Sweet and sour pork
铁板牛肉	Tiě bǎn niú ròu	Sizzling beef and onions
土豆烧牛肉	Tǔ dòu shāo niú ròu	Stewed beef and potatoes
宫宝鸡丁	Gōng bào jī dīng	Spicy chicken and peanuts
腰果鸡丁	Yāo guǒ jī dīng	Diced chicken and cashews
柠檬鸡	Níng méng jī	Lemon chicken
西红柿炒鸡蛋	Xī hóng shì chǎo jī dàn	Stir-fried eggs and tomatoes
蒜茸西兰花	Suàn róng xī lán huā	Stir-fried broccoli & garlic
蒜茸荷兰豆	Suàn róng hé lán dòu	Stir-fried snow peas & garlic
蛋炒饭	Dàn chǎo fàn	Egg fried rice
面条	Miàn tiáo	Noodles
可口可乐	Ké kǒu ké lè	Coca-cola
雪碧	Xuě bì	Sprite

APPENDIX B: Some Place Names

机场	jī chǎng	airport
火车站	huǒ chē zhàn	train station
医院	yī yuàn	hospital
公园	gōng yuán	park
地铁站	dì tiě zhàn	subway station

APPENDIX C: Countries and Cities (English-speaking)

Měi guó	美国	United States
Jiā ná dà	加拿大	Canada
Aō dá lì yā	澳大利亚	Australia
Yīng guó	英国	England (Great Britain)
Xīn xí lán	新西兰	New Zealand

APPENDIX D: Some Important Chinese Characters

These are some common and useful characters that you should learn to recognize. They may come in handy!

男	nán	man (male)
女	nǚ	woman (female)
厕所	cè suǒ	toilet
出口	chū kǒu	exit
入口	rù kǒu	entrance
禁止	jìn zhǐ	prohibited
银行	yíng háng	bank
医院	yī yuàn	hospital
学校	xué xiào	school
超市	cháo shì	supermarket

APPENDIX E: Beijing Polite

Greetings and Introductions / Leave-taking

- Formal introductions are important.
- Stand when being introduced. Remain standing until everyone is directed to sit down.
- Good ice-breaking conversation topics include: food, weather, hobbies, travel, sports, family
- Shaking hands is common. For women it is best to wait for the other person to extend the handshake first, and then respond.
- Use both hands to give / receive business cards.
- When a guest is leaving your home or office, escort them to the door. If it is a more formal situation, then you should escort them to the street.
- If someone enters your home or office, you must offer them something to drink (water, tea, etc.). Chinese etiquette demands that they decline the offer, but that you continue offering until you eventually give it to them. Even if they are thirsty, they will refuse. Give them something anyway.
- Likewise, if you are offered something to drink in an office or home, the polite response is to refuse, even if

you are dying of thirst. Don' t worry; they' ll give you something anyway.

Social Distance, Touching, Gestures

- Don' t hug, slap a person' s back, or put your arm around a person.
- Remember that China is very crowded and your western sense of personal space will be greatly reduced.

Gift-giving

- Give / receive gifts with two hands.
- When you give a wrapped gift to a Chinese person, don' t expect him/her to open it in your presence.
- When you are given a wrapped gift, do not open it in the presence of the giver.

Dining and Banqueting

- There are strict rules governing who sits where at a banquet, so you may not choose your own seat at a banquet table. Wait to be seated by your host.
- Leave some food on your plate to show that host that you are full. If you eat all of the food served it will imply that the host has not fed you enough.
- Do not place chopsticks in a bowl in a vertical position. This signifies the worship of the dead.
- A common expression when toasting is "gān bēi." This literally means "dry cup." A better translation is 'bottoms up,' or 'cheers.'
- A banquet ends when the host declares it to be finished. It is not polite to leave early.

APPENDIX F: Useful Pharmacy Terms

泰诺林	tài nuò lín	Tylenol
布洛芬	bù luò fēn	Ibuprofen
抗生素	kàng shēng sù	anti-biotics
青霉素	qíng méi sù	penicillin
抗组胺药	kàng zú ān yào	antihistamine
阿莫西林	ā mò xī lín	amoxycillan
酒精	jiǔ jīng	alcohol (methyl alcohol)
维生素	wéi shēng sù	vitamin C
氰化克的松	qīng huà kě de sōng	hydrocortisone
褪黑素	tuī heī sù	melatonin

APPENDIX G: A Hundred Fun Things to See and Do in Beijing

Whether you are visiting for a short time, or settling in for a longer stay, this list of 100 fun things to see and do in Beijing will help you get out and explore.

If you find yourself visiting (or living in) a city other than Beijing, this list can be a useful guide for you to explore that city. Many of the 'generic' activities would be the same (eating in various restaurants, enjoying the activities in a park, shopping in the local markets). Beyond that, you can develop your own list of museums, tourist sights, and local specialties.

1. Attend a Chinese Acrobats performance.
2. Attend a concert in the National Opera House.
3. Attend a folk or jazz concert at the Sanwei Bookstore.
4. Attend a Peking Opera.
5. Attend a show at the Lao She Teahouse.
6. Attend services at one of the Catholic Churches.
7. Attend services at one of the Protestant Churches.
8. Attend the flag raising/lowering ceremonies at Tiananmen Square (sunrise/sunset).

9. Climb the Great Wall at Jinshanling and hike to Simatai.

10. Climb to the top of Coal Hill in Jingshan Park (just north of the Forbidden City).

11. Climb up the mountain then ride down the alpine slide at Badachu Park.

12. Dance with locals in the park in the morning or evening.

13. Drink 'bubble tea.'

14. Eat "Over the Bridge Noodles" at a Yunnan restaurant.

15. Eat a bowl of *zhá jiāng miān* (a Beijing noodle dish).

16. Eat at a "Beijing Hot-pot" restaurant.

17. Eat at an outdoor café in the lakes area (Houhai).

18. Eat at the Old Beijing Noodle Shop across from the Pearl Market

19. Eat *bāo zī* on the street for breakfast.

20. Eat Beijing Roast Duck.

21. Eat candied fruit on a stick (bingtang hulu).

22. Eat *jiānbing* on the street for breakfast.

23. Eat *jiǎozi* in a local noodle shop.

24. Eat lamb kabobs at a Xinjiang restaurant

25. Eat scorpions on a stick at the Wangfujing night market.

26. Eat snacks on the street in the evening.

27. Eat *yóutiáo* (oil sticks) on the street for breakfast.

28. Enjoy a tea ceremony at a teahouse.

29. Get a 'dry hair wash.'

30. Get a facial.

31. Get a foot massage.

32. Get a manicure/pedicure.

33. Go boating at Houhai.

34. Go boating at the Summer Palace.

35. Go to the top of the Gate of Heavenly Peace to look out over Tiananmen Square.

36. Go up into the tower at Deshengmen.

37. Hang out at The Village at Sanlitun (tons of Western restaurants; Apple Store).

38. Hang out in an exercise park.

39. Have a suit or dress made.

40. Rent a bike.

41. Ride a bus to the end of the line. Get off and explore.

42. Ride a subway to either end. Get off and explore.

43. Ride the alpine slide at Mutianyu Great Wall.

44. Ride the tourist express train from Xizhimen to the Badal-ing Great Wall.

45. See the pandas at the Beijing Zoo.

46. Shop at Beijing Glasses City (low priced frames and lenses).

47. Shop at Jenny Lou's imported foods market.

48. Shop at Jingwuxing Wholesale Market.

49. Shop at Ladies' Street.

50. Shop at Panjiayuan Antique Market.
51. Shop at the clothing wholesale market across from the Beijing Zoo.
52. Shop at the Pearl Market.
53. Shop at the Silk Market.
54. Shop at the wholesale fabric market at Muxiyuan.
55. Shop at the Yashow Market.
56. Shop at Tianyi Wholesale Market.
57. Shop for antique furniture and reproductions at Gaobeidian.
58. Shop for computers/electronics in Zhongguancun.
59. Shop in a morning market.
60. Shop in the Xidan area.
61. Sing Karaoke at a KTV establishment.
62. Take a boat ride along the canal to/from the Summer Palace.
63. Take a rickshaw tour of the old Hutong neighborhoods
64. Visit Beihai Park.
65. Visit Chuandixia Ming Village (2.5 hours west of town in the mountains).
66. Visit the 798 Art District (galleries and restaurants).
67. Visit the ancestral home of Lu Xun.
68. Visit the Ancient Music Center at Zhihua Temple.
69. Visit the Ancient Observatory at Jianguomen.
70. Visit the Beijing City Planning Exhibition.

71. Visit the Bell Tower and Drum Towers.

72. Visit the Big Bell Temple to view China's largest bell.

73. Visit the Botanical Gardens.

74. Visit the Capital History Museum.

75. Visit the CCTV Tower.

76. Visit the China Minorities Park.

77. Visit the Confucian Temple.

78. Visit the Forbidden City.

79. Visit the Fragrant Hills.

80. Visit the Great Hall of the People.

81. Visit the Great Hall of the People.

82. Visit the Mao Ze-dong Mausoleum.

83. Visit the Mausoleum of Chairman Mao at Tiananmen Square.

84. Visit the Military Museum.

85. Visit the Museum of Ancient Chinese Architecture

86. Visit the National Art Museum

87. Visit the Old City Wall at Chongwenmen, including Dongbianmen Tower

88. Visit the Old Summer Palace

89. Visit the Planetarium

90. Visit the site of 'Peking Man' in Zhoukoudian (Fangshan District)

91. Visit the Summer Palace

92. Visit the Temple of Heaven.

93. Visit the tomb of Matteo Ricci.

94. Visit the Water Cube.

95. Visit the Yonghegong Lama Temple.

96. Vist the Museum of Natural History.

97. Vist the Sackler Museum of Art and Archeology at Beijing University.

98. Wander along Nan Lou Gu Xiang (cafés and nightclubs).

99. Wander the old streets of the Da Zha Lan (Da Sha Lanr) district.

100. Wander the refurbished Qianmen Street.